Moving Out

The Virginia Commonwealth University Series
for Contemporary Poetry

Walton Beacham, General Editor

Moving Out

David Walker

University Press of Virginia

Charlottesville

THE UNIVERSITY PRESS OF VIRGINIA
Copyright © 1976 by the Rector and Visitors
of the University of Virginia

First published 1976

Library of Congress Cataloging in Publication Data

Walker, David, 1942-
  Moving out.

  (The Virginia Commonwealth University series for con-
temporary poetry)
  I. Title. II. Series: Virginia Commonwealth University.
The Virginia Commonwealth University series for contem-
porary poetry.   PS3573.A42533M6   811'.5'4   75-31971
ISBN 0-8139-0657-1

Printed in the United States of America

Foreword

David Walker's poetry is rich in old New England attitudes about ancestors, place, and conditions of life. He gives us mature realizations of life and death, and he possesses an acute historical sense. He is a profound man writing of deep things in a language that is central to English because it is hard, strong, and plain. His poetry is subjective and personal; yet it has a sense of the universal and of timeless values.

He might have retorted to Ezra Pound, who said "Make it New," make it old. It is not that he is controversial. He would do no such thing. I speak of an opposite wisdom which he has. He is not experimental in devising new linguistic methods. Rather, he senses man as an experiment of nature, and writes about ancient awarenesses which are also awarenesses of the present, of every day.

It is a poetry close to the earth, to the soil. His verbal adroitness grows on one. It is the central truth of his poems that is manifested as one comes to know their varieties of honesty, their recognition of the human condition, their hold on generalities, the niceties of their particularizations. While many of his poems are based on New England and Maine, one does not think of him as a local poet. He evokes feelings available to everybody.

These poems are not primarily philosophical nor do they present dogmatic platforms. They are not given to excesses nor to flamboyance. What, then, do they show? They show a wide range of life, of history, of being in the central part of man's life, the core realities of every man and woman. They are strong, of a rare kind of simplicity, and have deep realizations that make them seem like permanent parts of our knowledge. There is a unity throughout these poems, a depth of sameness of approach to many facets of living, suffering, and dying. The poet knows the people, his common people, farm people. He renders them so well that the reader is pleased with a sense of verisimilitude. Walker writes a kind of classic naturalism, "All History stalled down some abandoned road, / And Art a spinster sighting

along her thread / Till gossip knots half-truth by which it lives."
"The first snow of the year lights up the dark."

In "Plowing with Grandfather" the relationship to the horse is "A relationship / of perfect love and cussedness." This poetry close to the land, the land of Maine, expresses the integrity of farming, of the relationship of father and son, of many deep relationships, with delighting observations such as

> Yet how long
> The sun leaks from the grass, till in that shock
> It runs into an earth where green is black.

There are long historical poems going back to the sixteenth century and coming up to the nineteenth century. In "The Grandmother" he observes

> your man addled
> off to bed, but yourself more decent each day
> and each year, more alone.

He observes of an old man dying, in "The Grandfather," how he wanders out somewhere

> not questioning, not seeing the ground
> under your eyes, nor hearing the bird,
> wind, nor anything known to air,
> but listening inside to yourself, like a man
> so old, he is sounding his grave
> or stumbles, being yet a child.

And of sons, "sons would be takers / for the shrewd bargain of a past worth answering for." This is a stalwart New England view lost on many youths today, a character reminder.

In this book are poems of Scotland, Bavaria, to Chateaubriand, to Keats, to Shelley, for Osip Mandelstam, poems of Gettysburg, The Meuse-Argonne Campaign, 1918, to his wife, and here is one to his daughter which shows his wisdom:

I. A Prayer, A Welcome

> Little wrinkle
> from my flesh, eyelid

curling down at my fool's
prattle; child

before whom I'm the more
child—your future

older than my past. . . .
Forgive the father

I'll be, become all
I can never know;

teach me to hold
you for a while, and then

to let go.

His poems to his grandfather, his father, and other ancestors, remind me of Nicolai Fyodorov, the Russian philosopher of the late nineteenth century, known to Tolstoy and Dostoevski, whose ideas are only now becoming widely known. He held that the trouble with Western civilization is that it lost belief in the father and that only when we learn the meaning of fatherhood will civilization prosper.

Perhaps the true word to say of Walker's poems is that they are stoical. To be stoical is to know much and expect little. Within the stoical attitude, central to New England consciousness, David Walker gives us his rich and memorable poems. This loam is fertile. When so much poetry is limited to intellectual brilliance here is a young poet with strength of character, deep knowledge of history and nature, who writes from the heart as well as the head to give us fullness and wholeness of life.

RICHARD EBERHART

Acknowledgments

The author and publisher wish to thank the following magazines for permission to reprint certain poems:

The *Antioch Review* for "Sir Ferdinando Gorges Relates the Discovery of the Sheepscot River" (originally "One Sir Fernando Gorges Discovereth the Sheeps Cot River: Spring, 1608"). Copyright 1970 by The Antioch Review, Inc. First published in *The Antioch Review*, vol. 30, no. 1, p. 68; reprinted by permission of the editors.

Bartleby's Review for "The Beast of Burden"

Concerning Poetry for "In August" and "For Osip Mandelstam"

Edge (New Zealand) for "Father and Son: Christmas Morning, 1967"

The *Georgia Review* for "The Talisman" (originally "The Paw"), "The Grandmother," "The Grandfather," "The Drowned Man," and "Chill from Sunlight." Copyright © 1969 by the University of Georgia. Reprinted by permission of *The Georgia Review*.

Hellcoal Annual #2 for "Keats: The First Hemorrhage" and "The Death of Shelley"

The *Maine Sunday Telegram* for "For Emma, at Sunrise" and "My Grandfather's Wooden Planes"

The *Maine Times* for "The Peaceable Kingdom," "The Naming," "The Source," "Spring in the Pennines" (originally "Maine Spring"), "Union Cavalry on Leave," "Mare Night," and "Private Beach"

The *New Yorker* for "The Crossing," p. 3, and "Baptism: Maine, 194-," p. 4 (originally "A Baptist Church in Maine"), © 1968 & 1971, The New Yorker Magazine, Inc.

Northwest Review for "Fragment from a Last Letter Home" (originally "Two Fragments from a Last Letter Home") and "Two Seasons" (originally "Two Seasons [1950]")

The *Ohio University Review* for "Testament for an Old Lady"

Perspective for "Bavarian Pinewoods, September" (originally "Pinewoods in August")

Poetry for "Homing" and "The Farmer's Son"

Poetry Northwest for "In the Northern Lakes: Early Spring, 1830" and "Advice for a Family Historian"

The *Poetry Review* (England) for "Saint Mary's Loch, Scotland"

Presumpscot for "For My Daughter before Dawn," "Reflections on Proverbs," "New England Backcountry," and "In the Slaughterhouse"

Seneca Review for "Ancestral Photograph" and "Berlioz 1830" (originally "The Lover: Paris, 1830")

Southern Poetry Review for "The Guilt" and "Plowing with Grandfather"

Transatlantic Review for "Light Lines for My Father"

West Coast Poetry Review for "Seasons of Passage" (originally "Seasons")

The author wishes to thank the Corporation of Yaddo for a period of residence during which work on this book was completed.

Contents

To cut away from the past . . . to annihilate it, is the vilest of all breaches of the laws of the cosmos. It is ingratitude, and running away from your debt. It is suicide. . . . I shall not, at the moment when I have become, truthfully, what I am, in cutting off my roots turn myself into a shadow, into nothingness.

—Isak Dinesen, "A Country Tale"

For M:

Praise to her under my arm
in the waystations of sleep:
bound in my every limb,
firm in my darkest step.

I: *Homing*

Tasten über die grünen Stufen des Sommers
—Georg Trakl, "Sebastian im Traum"

The Crossing

At the far edge of the field, just in the shade,
my father waves; the heat cuts us in two
as I walk towards him. The stubble bleeds
yellow, then nearly white; it crunches like snow.

Into the sun I stride, erect in my cause
and body straining towards the other side.
Hands on his hips, my father watches me cross
calmly. I am revolved in the season's eye.

The sun leans in the distance, drawing a cloak
of pines slowly over its head; and still
he is waiting. Every year that I walk
his smile grows nearer. And I begin to smile.

Baptism: Maine, 194–

Sunday . . . the bells toll "White!
white!" on the robin's-egg June sky;
they summon to the voice of God
made flesh and unordained—a back-road
spawner of sermons and daughters. His face
by ten o'clock sweats upon its smile,
his fat hands suffer and bless
the cowed, anemic children who pile
with powdered and hair-slicked parents from old Fords,
Chevies, and Ben Crockett's '47
Kaiser, pink as a new ribbon.

The First Baptist Church
was the only straight way I'd get the Word,
Grandfather said. After his stroke,
he sat propped up by the starch in his shirts,
unable to speak.

I wanted to touch
the bell ropes like braided tails;
at each pull,
a monster cow in the steeple
bellowed, her cry slopping over
the close hills and bouncing off the river;
but the bells belonged to the young Gordons,
their father a black-suited deacon
and used-car dealer.
Each Sunday, they drove up in a different model.

*

At sunset, twenty years later,
the peeling, off-white spire's
a monument that sinks three inches each year,

4

its people
backsliders as well. . . .

Moonrise . . . the last Baptist hillbilly,
eyelids raw from whiskey,
will appear seeking the rough hand, the chill
waters. Will lie
all night on the steps' moss-stained
granite, crying
for the misplaced, obsolescent damned.

Chill from Sunlight

What's that man up to, who telescopes the moon
through the wrong end of an empty whiskey bottle?
All afternoon, hunched on the back-porch rocker,
he's paced the white heat with a darker fire,
amber against mere dazzle; yet each measure
at time dandled jauntily over stone steps
from a slack hand—calloused, tanned, but the veins
an uncertain chalk, a tic like lightning. And always
the muttering over whatever brought him there:
not women, but the land a little, or the same
dream of all-splintering sun as charmed one cousin
to burn a barn down over his stock and crops.

So this: who'd have worked things out
but for lack of room or light; who makes widening pleas
of arm and head, foot-tap become a kicking,
till the whole body, spelled to its spot, casts out
as against the sunset its devils, with a crying
whether of rage—as the shadows, the last, lick
closer to his feet—or more, of sorrow: not
for a love lost in night, but for fire downed
so that nothing's left to match the moon's chill, nothing
to drain like a glass with the cunning fit for age.

New England Backcountry

Wind furls the pinetops, hauls up the blinding salt
As a final catch. . . . You found no seaward house
But dipped almost to its weeds a shuttered loss:
Goldenrod spreading like cancer, and the silt
Rusted before the plow; stray bones of a carriage
Leprous with swallow stains in the barn past salvage. . . .

Dead-water sideshow, revised these hundred years
Less than the moon: farmer and fisherman thinning
To ruin still in the backwash of old wars,
Both coast and upland blank to the cold stars' burning.

So a spare gift can deplore the thing it loves:
All History stalled down some abandoned road,
And Art a spinster sighting along her thread
Till gossip knots half-truth by which it lives.

Two Seasons
(of 1950)

I. *Midsummer: The Market Gardener*

Water jets from the hose and smacks the canvas
over the cooling sweet corn:
                    Seven A.M.;
in an hour half the truckload will have been sold.

Still drenched in sleep as in sweat, my father
slumps in gumboots.... A new calf sways to its feet,
the sun leaning heavily on its back.

II. *The Day After Thanksgiving*

The cattle driven in, I latch the door;
but they still dance
the flakes like fish scales off their startled backs.

Behind them, behind us all,
outside but certain of its welcome,
the first snow of the year lights up the dark.

8

In the Slaughterhouse
(1953)

Packed in the sawdust, layer on layer,
Block-ice it took two men to cut
And a team to grapple, turned to air
And water. . . . Blue, still crammed with light,

These ornaments seemed out of season;
Or so a boy of ten assumes
In spring, using a summer's reason.
Each night, their sweat ticked through my dreams

Like some mad clockwork.
                    What they told,
I learned on the evening thoughtful men
Worked by the lamp they let me hold:
A bull calf trembling in a pen;

A sling hung level with my head,
Rich leather gleaming; mallets, knives
And a pan. . . .Their eyes gauged how it bled:
Half-slumped, as though still half-alive

After the stroke. . . .
                    And then I heard
The metronome that kept their time:
Black ice that dripped without a word
But as the blood slowed, seemed to chime.

Plowing with Grandfather

I.   1954

I lead the white horse, Captain,
or else the black horse, Colonel
who is wild:

red eyes socketed
in fear, the tendrilous nostrils
sucking through the hum of blowflies

(once, when thrown,
to feel the back of my skull
like an open flap. . . .)

Green-drench
of teeth corroding the bit,
and my hand on the checkrein

turning into moss.

*

A tobacco mustache
to the roots, its stained gray

straggling the tanned jaw
and cheekbones (a web of veins. . . .)

Walking the horses, his body
drags: a stubborn plumbstone between them

as they toss
heads, snort, do their little dance

carefully avoiding his toes.
A relationship

of perfect love and cussedness.

              *

Hooves
rile the cinders—less furrows
than an overcooked crust

even in May. I grit
my teeth on grit, hearing it settle
in my ears, my hair
                     (the plowblade

snags—then grates
painfully over a stone. . . .)
                  But damn it!
the old man sweet-talks

the horses, sasses
back at a bossy crow—from under
his straw hatbrim, he keeps up

his droning all summer: a ten years' sleep.

II. *November 1964*

Hung in the damp shed, the harnesses
rot and the metal snaps

rust shut; the fat, brass spangles
dull and the blue-glass

11

ornaments cloud over
or splinter; the chips dwindling

through shadowed crevices the frost
springs wider each year. . . .

Their facets blackened, flawed from the cold,
those last, shining bits will burn out

under my feet.

Homing

I. *The Farmer's Son*

My father is dying while the breast-high fields
Sway in a sea of light this heat of June:
Bowed to their ripening like silent girls,
They fold themselves in greenness one by one.

The shining trees are teethed with bark; the scythe
Falls through the heavy day.... Before the blade
Of lightning lashes out and reaps the earth
To dusk, I run for the last light were we stood

And talked in May: he told me then what fire
Works like a barb in every deepening thing,
How water mates by drowning and the air
Confounds all death with marriage.
                                             Yet how long
The sun leaks from the grass, till in that shock
It runs into an earth where green is black.

II. *The Farmer before Winter*

By scavenge wedded to the ground
In rain that picks November's bones,
I burn on the wind's whistling blade
And watch my veins redden to clay;

And hush for the distant plunge of deer
Whose crippled leap must run a bare
Gauntlet—the thorn edged like a curse—
To graze upon a pool of rust.

13

My springtime courted with the earth
Till harvest dulled the whetted scythe
I trail, still shining, home through the mud
Like antlers cast in undergrowth:
A ring to summon what dark bride?

III. *Homing*

Now when the plowed land browns,
heavy with fall, I turn
with the arching of long furrows—
the deliberate heir of thorn and stone.

I lie with the broken harrow's wheel,
with the horse's whitening thigh,
in the dominion of crows scouring
the earth, the bare winds and my eyes.

I see the sky clouded with horses
dashing the air, spilling
ice in runnels of an oak, skimming
silent pools of departed birds.

The apples drop and fire in the grass. . . .
I smoulder for their sight;
I cry to break this sleep. And break
the frost, but find my tongue a root.

Father and Son: Christmas Morning, 1967

Woolly, withdrawn yet curious,
the Herefords breathing blocks of ice
huddle, stamping, by the truck: their child's
round eyes, needled by the cold.
                                    And while
we pitch them bales, you punctuate
effort with reckoning our estate
and ancestry: whimsical, yet grave
as a showman geared to routine, you wave
vaguely with the fork—"that cornerstone
of the old barn, lugged there by someone:
Abiel? Abraham?" And I gaze,
squinting, along your pointed steel;
straining to recognize the real
that's blacked out, almost, in this blaze
of surreally blue December air,
with everything too clearly there
to be sure of . . . while my hands prickle
for the ice now sliding from a shingle
that smokes in the sun. Once the universe
moved here, once the land for miles was ours.

By the road's rim, above our heads,
cars speed, the cold tar burning from treads
that squeal, gambling on a grip:
their stakes, a perpetual life trip. . . .

I turn back to the keystoned arch
of granite, the barn's core; I search
far out of sunlight into that dark
where the stock can flee, as to an Ark,
our boding climate (investment's risk).
I wonder, Father, but do not ask
where I might shelter in time to come:
what hope shall keystone my own home
when you've resigned from the land you keep
to be kept by it, and the miles are sleep. . . .

"They built this place. . . ." Your last words freeze,
you brace—and the last bale arcs against trees
and falls where the shaggy yearlings browse
forward through hoarfrost, snow: eyes closed
from dazzle to pleasure as they devour
their manna—not guessing what growth is for.

Our engine races; braced to its churn
and whine—an excuse for silence—we turn
homeward, eyes slit for the sun: poor, stark
last link of its own descent, to burn
downward and out each day — the spark
of dynasty, freezing. Till our sight goes dark.

The Talisman

There was a tangle once I had to go back to:
barbed wire rotten against the snow,
the dark tines straggling in a thicket
like the stain of apples caving under frost.

For in the deepest knot, the most intricate
twining of cold iron with spoor of rust,
a paw hung: though whose bleached fur and delicate
bones, I could hear no echo around to ask.

It swung there, undeniable, all that winter
in the wind: bloodless, yet speaking to me of blood
and a cry long frozen beyond my answer
where the ghost of metal hugged to its strange food.

II: *Ancestors*

... it has been the destiny of successive generations to struggle with wars and difficulties reiterated and uncommon, and to wade through sufferings deep and indescribable.
—Williamson, *History of Maine*

Advice for a Family Historian

Call back the past, and you evoke those dead
whose courses will evade responsible blessing,
unless run to ground; and then, like the blaze of tracks
in spring crossing a field, will trail off at the last
on a granite rib where inheritors lose the scent.
Or just when you think the air murmurs of portent,
become the mumble of vacancy, sheer sky.

I advise those who would follow to the end—
if any from love, patience or mulishness
shall have struggled thus far—to bide until moonlight;
or best, till a night so racked with its rain and cold,
even the stones are beside themselves, and the great trees
rooted only in fear. Then with no light, nor word
but your blood racing for signal, strike out
for a place—not a house or the well-kept grave,
but more circumspect: your own body will guide you
strangely to the spot, your feet stumbling as you begin
almost to run. Until maybe some half-rotten post,
edged in the black by a halo of white phosphorous,
warns you are there—found at the heart of the storm
by this most neutral, forgotten and daylight-dull
of shaped things.
          Desire of motion now lost,
spilt on air and the arguing elements you may learn
you were born for this, as far back as you can hear,
through the dark, this wood sharpened by an ax
dogged with love—a man building a fence,
a son and the son's sons, not blindly
but growing beyond foreknowledge of their decay.

Sir Ferdinando Gorges Relates the Discovery of the Sheepscot River (Spring 16--)

Our longboat pulling through the blazon of afternoon,
we probed upriver, took soundings for a mile
above the bay: sandbars a yellow roil
two fathoms down, and shifting slow with the tide
as a brassy cloud troubled before storm winds. . . .
One rock split the passage, but the short lead gave us
clear channel by lee-side; we forced that narrows
with a smallsword's length to spare, and soon
in still water, limpid as a deer's eye
or the teardrop of a Queen, set anchor.

Becalming the pine tops, a hush as of wings enfolded
our foreign shapes and colors: specks on that mirror
reflecting heaven and framed by green profusion.
An unbaited hook found chub, Atlantic salmon,
and one lifted the Great Blue Trout, his gills
flecked with a blood the sun transformed to orange.
Our skin there, flayed by a coppery sky, became
first raw as the slit fish, then a savage brown
till we looked not of our country, and gazed unsure
unto whose land we came—by what pale title
on which cramped hands had dashed a little ink?

Thus we rested, silent, over oars: till the thwarts creaked
gently to warn us, the day's last turning tide
now funeled downstream: pouring us towards night.
We shot the narrows too close, and once the keel
scraped on a boulder hairy with moss — its back
acrust with barnacles like some ancient tortoise . . .
while the light dipped, then went out amid the pine
and spruce: though still blinking through gaps
like forty eyes, or forty golden coins.

Sir Ferdinando Gorges

As then we pulled for the black smudge of our ship
on a crimson sky, our flag beyond haven's holding,
I saw our blades sink into velvet pile
and winnow pearls that, scattering, fell back
to be lost from sight in deeps no lead might fathom. . . .

Owls mocked from the hills; overhead, the wind
drove down on us insects that hummed and clustered
stickily on blistered skin. And when, adrift
as a blanched week on the dusk, the Huntress Moon
brushed over us, I watched how she carved the bones
of our faces silver, but hollow, and burned the skulls
to their white sockets chased with sweat like tears.

Aground
(A Settler's View, Maine, 17th C.)

Our boat strikes first on tideflats, then a waste
of boulders: round, but slippery to heft
and slime underfoot like moss—the bowling green
of Hell? The banks above grow eel grass, matted
riff raff cast by the tide—a clay-daubed stick
signing our New Found Land.... I trap my last
ship's louse, triumphant, while a bird screams loud
in a strange tree; our minister hacks, spits brown.
Ahead, the woods tell nothing I can sift.

Now a barge pulls toward the salt marsh, bearing the thick
hulks of our bellowing oxen: old-world, sly,
they balk both hoof and muzzle at the greener shores
and pastures of our need. Though He smell the blood
where gnats have stung them, yet shall The Lord provide:
He prods them through our sharp goads, lest we die.

Red through the black woods also now, the sun
declines. We huddle, gazing blind at guttering fires,
then bargain chill for rest while the watches stare
all night into the river drained by stars.
After a cramped sleep, Lord, we pray You steer
our westering through this undergrowth at dawn.

The Bridal
(1782)

In 1771, according to family tradition, Abraham Walker lay with
an Indian girl who later bore him a son. However, he never saw
the girl again, and never met his child.

(from a work-in-progress)

. . . . .

The girl at the pool was there before I knew
I was there, and not dropped into a dream,
a wry trick of the heat and my fruitless nights.
I blessed my woodscraft on intake of breath
not to have been seen, by her or anyone,
sprung on such nakedness; but sank where I stood,
of a sudden cool, and fever a moment stilled
by contemplation. I might have been a saint,
though already the blood was drumming in my head
how I'd more crafts than one: how adoration
was a playing possum, to give me time to plan.

Veiled only by heat, blue veins tilted the nipples
upward, two faint bruises against the brown;
the belly, a sheet of velvet, plateaued downward
to a darkness, with the hairs that guarded the cleft
water-combed, drying to curls in the sun.
On a warm bank, eyes shut, spread to the air
with one arm thrown back, the other grazing her thigh,
and one foot still swaying half in the water. . . .
Fullness that all men dream of, but born from what?
Crocodiles' eggs, slime as our ministers said:
the bastard spawn of some French whore in scarlet,
the Nigger Pope, Cannibals of th'Antipodes;
what more not call them, in a righteous war where the guns
go primed with the Word as with shot—
                                    and yet
fullness of The Lord lay there, and in His garden;
what use to turn it to, when man and the serpent
confuse—till only the crooked way is straight?

25

So the White God passed through her sun a moment
over the grass, his clothes like an old faith
lost in the trampled leaves. So when I lowered
myself upon her, her waking to cries, to scratch
and kick, twisting her limbs like an eel
against me, seemed also planned—a striving
that worked more towards than apart, till soon
mouth closed over mouth, tongue mingled with tongue
and something unseen yet probing surely home
like a great trout finding his lair, exploded rings
in the sea made sun—a drowning also burning.

But read in forbidden poets of those delights
told as by conquerors, leching over maps
of the worlds they've been, or as some fumbling priest
gone randy over his beads. Enough that our world
lay there an hour, that a lifetime of begetting
the furtive children who'll fail to warm your house
showed childish to this—a something I could hold
by a sure gladness now, as well for a day
or the next hard years: a core of some private humor.
As Warren said, I'd act as if something droll
kept watchful in me, shy of being said out,
but worth hearing if ever it was. I let him think
what he couldn't know, as I let Parson Bates talk God
over grace, and racier after some spirits.
"One thing about Walker here; he's never loud,"
said Warren, and "It augurs well," Bates rumbled
"in a young man. Meanwhile, pass God's bounty"
—meaning the bottle.

·   ·   ·   ·   ·

The Bridal

I wanted—I want—not even that one girl:
outside of her sex and youth, some dirty Indian
now probably running to fat. And it's not
the new nation, or freedom—who can taste that "free"?—
but maybe, at thirty, the start of a new chase
not only not lost, but not yet gone mazed and dark.
I want—say it out, clear for once—my youth
even if confused, God-ridden, secret in a sin
its own flesh might dissolve, if shaken into light
by that fullness again: the dark girl turning in the light
as her gutturals stung me, the flail and tussle
of limbs; and the soul wrenched free, forced to find room. . . .

The mind dickers with sin, or absence of sin
from this earth; the body's lashed to the plow;
and the soul a toss-up between them, or drowned in rum.
A white woman bleaches indoors and bears
like spitting seeds; her hands knot in a prayer
for you—that is, for herself: shutting you out.

But it's not the woman; no, nor even being young.
Only something about that day, the sun
flat to the grass, or curling along a belly
falling to hair . . . the white and the brown mingling,
and four eyes watching: or shut, holding their peace
as though far more than a child might come to pass
and more than two languages mix on darted tongues. . . .

Oh call it what you like; only, know something
came, fairer than the day: as out of the ground—
when stones turn upward, basking in the new year—
like a man the first sun wakes out of his house,
the grass snake comes to shed his scales, their rings
cast like a rainbow on the leaves, on air—
how blessed that dispossession for its hour.

27

The Drowned Man
(1796)

I, Abraham Walker, long safely dead,
now speak of what befell me that last December.

A starving fall had harried our crops; on its tail,
the first blizzard making, but lakes not yet sheeted over
when I struck out from the house, from the five
children and a still-young bride. I was after buck,
but pursued only phantoms all through that day;
alluring, yet insubstantial as the rustle of leaves,
the prints left cast in the cold like bronze.

So, myself spent but the gun still charged, near dark
coming home, the storm dropped down on me
sudden as a hood, and with a careless haste
unknown to me, I slipped out of my way
though soon my feet told the level of river ice.
The world, or what was left me, had turned to a mist
till, at the end of ice, a black ribbon
cracked up from the white—unwound on its clean sheet
a lightning instant, as if somehow I had walked
across blank sky: a floor impossible
except to one traveling, as I was,
out of this poor, flat world.
                              The mind cold
yet throbbing as though from whiskey, my boots
filling head over heels, I clutched at what I prayed
were buck's horns—they became twigs; I cried
for my wife, and she came to be sewn in black;
while groping me downward, deep as the undertow,
my father's hands brushed past my cheek like silt.
At the last came my children, whispering,
but I could not hold their words, that slipt through my arms
like water—
                  like the warm cry from my throat
driven upwards, tracking the bright farms
of the Great Bear on through years of unending snow.

In the Northern Lakes: Early Spring, 1830
(As Told by Benjamin Walker, Age Twenty)

That night, hearing the ice break up
out of sight from land, I felt wind from the arctic
pass by my fire, bringing first the ragged
volleys of the small rifts, like sleet on the panes
of my window at home, then the clash of the main floes
in a jagged thunder. And thrall to the dark
bothering my green fire with a breath
cold, tainted by the spring damps, I thought I heard
something approaching, that loped across the ice
with quick strides, yet seemed to grapple for hours
at each few feet; and I harkened to tales
of bears wounded, on bellies dragging overland
a yard at a time to reach the healing waters.

Two hundred feet straight up, the pines shuttled
the night across their boughs. I was alone,
I knew great Ursa nearer than the stars
bent down, and his blood made increment of ice
to be revealed, at the dawn, a frozen sunset
or false rainbow trapped in the shifting mirror. . . .
Everything stirred; only I did not breathe,
eyes ears and all senses strung beyond my age
to an old man's waiting for the figure, white
against nothing, whose arms shall unfold him a black
cry, his last of sound.
                    Till a firelog leapt
like a sprung trap, to fall drowsily back
in a blanket of sparks—flock of familiar stars
alighted on the snow. And I sank back
and filled with sleep as though with my spoken name,
rested upon my bones as about a weapon.

Ancestral Photograph
(c. 1860)

Dark is darker, and the white
startling as snow in the face
my great-grandfather thrusts
in the sculpturing light; his bones
have the harsh planes of the Indian-
head nickel's Indian, his clothes
are stovepipes fresh from the blacking.

His gaze outfaces the camera's;
one shrewd hand cups
a blazing kneecap, the other
is stuffed in his waistcoat as over
a wound. . . . The curl of his lips
mutters, "They got me" in nervous
defiance: now captive, the last
aristocratic New England peasant.

The Grandmother

You learn in the long room: people are something
done to you, they come and go like the clouds
so that sometimes you remark, "What a fair day,"
meaning no one called. Other times, you feel
the reins of your mind go taut at a strange voice,
foot-tread, or the creak of breathing; anything
to lock you up! Why did they have to come
outrageous as bad weather, set a damp in you
lasting all evening. On edge as the jug's
broken out, the men conniving against
your house: guffaws at a deal table
cramping yourself and all order
into an ill-lighted corner with the sewing,
but trembled too much to thread a needle.
Till they go whooping into the night, their dogs
baying them home, leaving you to cradle
the bones of your slighted world; your man addled
off to bed, but yourself more decent each day
and each year, more alone.

Testament for an Old Lady
(For A. J. W.)

As I practice dying, and into my thin darkness
crowd lights and relations—a shrill chorus,
pretending that there is still hope — I pray
that the wax smiles would melt, and I be left
to consider alone.
                    What I would see
in my mind then, the final landscape
of either world, is a field whose edges
curve upward, delaying the blank thrust of the sky
on all sides. A few maples, perhaps,
marking the center; but bare, and the autumn grasses
tawny, spiked with frost. No green anywhere;
and on the grassblades, that would raise themselves
for my inspection, the sawtooth ribbons
of ice, their facets shifting. But not yet melting;
I would hold them there awhile, in my eye's noon.

And nothing in that field would ever go dark
or move, except the soft hiss of the wind
at times I chose. Then at moments the grasses
might click together, just aloud, in the sun
that would be white; and I would be dressed in white
and come there to stir them with my breath,
to force brown crystal packed around the stems
relent its diamond will for me. For me!

The Grandfather

It feels good, an old man dried by the sun,
to sit still the long afternoons
and feel sleep trying to fill your head
with odd notions, such as which side
the dreams are on: before, or behind your eyes.
A crow, shimmering through the heat-haze:
or an eyelid, now. Or if a bird
cries out, why not talk to yourself
in foreign cries, perhaps, and rock your bones
past tears, in a joy too far
and personal for anyone's ears—
unsettling, even, to yours,
that have lived with common sounds
so long, and made the best of them; whereas this,
this seems some language never learmed on earth
though maybe beneath it; so that waking,
you rise slowly—for all your years
and the hot afternoon—and start off somewhere
not questioning, not seeing the ground
under your eyes, nor hearing the bird,
wind, nor anything known to air,
but listening inside to yourself, like a man
so old, he is sounding his grave
or stumbles, being yet a child.

The Peaceable Kingdom

Rain and October dusk. . . . Drawn to the house
they left, I lock the weather outside and fumble
for a light; but brush instead the radio
alive to a driving blues—as though some animal
awoke, lashing the room with cries.
                                        I look
for something to close with, recall by name,
but learn only the walls: how they're scrubbed bone-white,
naked as goodness; or the rocker, tipped
a little forward, sedate, as if someone worked
his sternness out there, turning it into a smile
gone stiff at the hinge. . . .
                        Preparation of bread:
hands gripping a hymnbook while the dough rises
and the stocks soar, yet lie in the safe that's black
as the Bible; and love like a fist, payed out
till its blows weakened the rafters, and the spread
demure curtains swelled with more than the wind.
Then sagging, a sourness: the children married off
to become a note at Christmas, and the Word
at last too brittle for speech: like the sheets, once
dazzling to the bride, wrung later my mottled hands
or silently piled to yellow on a dark shelf. . . .

I turn to go; spotted undersides of leaves
grapple and rasp at the window, then drop off
sudden as the throttled music—or as the door
thrusting me now at the rain's repeated cadence
that drums into the earth, yet twines with the night
its rods of monotone: the thicket of prayer.

The Family Burial Ground in April

Silt shining as the year recovers
scars, the trampled leaves sprung again,
I follow the lane; a bare coffin's
span threading stone wall, juniper,
the cool corridor of pine and fern
to the graveyard. While the season turns
I come to be measured by stone.

Here lie the God-fearing whose tongues
ran in odd corners, their gossip keyed
to bundling and bouts of the hard
applejack: the kindled eyes, flayed
by the Maine sleet, spill under coins
and the ears, whatever beasts or demons
they heard, are tucked beneath ragged stones.

Sunlight splayed by the branches
flashes like teeth—a sliding grin
for the damned who slave, spelling the moon
with foxfire that leaps at night
from logs: by their natural light
the dead finally shall dance, and headstones
crack the skulls of the righteous.

So when leaves crackle in the wind,
my scalp recalls those last redmen
Great-grandfather damned with shot,
liquor and predestination.
Truly he cleared enough this land,
driving buck and boar like unicorn
before his civil ax. I wait;

Judgment Day, will their plunge rend
the undergrowth, their nostrils burn
for my scent? Deep in this plot
the dead planted skills before I was born;
groping through time, I must kneel again
where last year's leaves cover the light —
the untarnished glint of the huntsman's horn.

Light Lines for My Father

March winds and a cold rain slant across the field
where the fence stakes smoke with wet and begin to rot—
blackened, almost adrift upon tides of silt—
till your real estate glooms like some vacant lot

no one would want to buy, and your love of earth
is the question mark of hands turning up your collar,
or is cast like smoke rings on disheartened breath
to be signed away for a few unghostly dollars.

Father, whose land? Let our ghostlier fathers answer;
signing their deeds with a gambler's luck for sons,
their canny flesh bred and bequeathed a future
kept solvent by sweat, fertility and loans

till unto our day they spread these rainlit acres
as a winning hand, come taxes depression or war
in the faith that—chill and all—sons would be takers
for the shrewd bargain of a past worth answering for.

III. *Elsewhere and Back*

And I say to you: when someone goes someone remains. The point where a man passed is no longer alone. . . . The steps, the kisses, the pardons, the crimes have gone. What continues in the house is the foot, the lips, the eyes, the heart. Negations and affirmations, good and evil, have scattered. What continues in the house is the subject of the act.

—César Vallejo, "No vive nadie en la casa"
(trans. Clayton Eshleman)

Landscapes

I. *Saint Mary's Loch, Scotland*

These trees such as they stand—thumbs down
on the earh, ruminating dry stones—
have no need to grow old, being born old.
And no soil relents, used to be manhandled;
each cliff's a hag, thrusting her breast
abrupt to the slavering weathers.

The wind here sings no creature to rest,
and no bird flowers
save some few black familiars:
the hawks breeding on a sky of rust.

No grass but a congress of weeds, of heather
gone out like a dead star; the stream
beds fouled,
    while the air—circling—takes aim
and will neither conciliate nor clear:

here is small time to learn,
before you go under,
how at once to hang on and bow down.

II. *Spring in the Pennines*

White rivers poured out on roads,
and the roads fields.

Till a brown track wears through:
the ridge—mud and flintcrop—
of the world's sullen spine.

Then dried-blood ochres, patching
the oceans of silt . . . and the green tuft-islands
rising from those dead honeycombs,
the hoarfrosted tussocks.

At sunset, a single stone
gathers the light: its quartz eye
stares upward, dividing the dark waters.

III. *Bavarian Pinewoods, September*

Sweat from my face comes off in my hands
like soot; when I rub my eyes, the blue pines
are ground out in splinters.
                          The air
burns white with the pungent tears of resin; the wind's
absorbed into light.

I'm no one: I cling
to a blazing stump while dry fingers explore
my skull—the fall of needles sifting
over unfleshed bone.

The Man at the Edge

I. *Chateaubriand at the Hunt*
                    (1788)

Crystal the morning of hooves
drumming on frost, stone; the hare
screams, the bolt twangs from the groove
and bleeds the morning. . . . Our sire
the Comte—in frogged coat, his hand
boned finer than a squirrel's
wishbone rib—is riding honed
to his prerogative: tall
as his thoughts, while the eyes gaze
inward on vacancy; on the white
shimmer of uniforms, all
uniform. . . . The clay hovels
a blur, then lost: below his notice,
whose ritual is their fate.

II. *Keats: The First Hemorrhage*

Nothing . . . then a spot, and then
another spot—the sunset
ebbing through snow, through the sheet
whiter than his girl's wrist, than
her yards of dazzling tulle: "to
me an object intensely
desirable—"
                    the pen's grate
now frozen; its slow-motion
colors seeping through black to
brown to. . . .
                    Lovely, the phrase wrung
(unsuitable for poetry)
from the once-failed medico:
"arterial blood," that cockney
learning: vengeance of breeding.

43

III. *The Death of Shelley*

Still shuffling off the heat
of the day like rust, the boy-god
Icarus, his arms a liquid
bronze, his stare rapt with the need
to fall. . . .
            Then Lerici: green bay,
boat cruising water so still,
the mast reflected its full
twenty feet, a plumb line. . . . Then the sky
racked, and the quick god flaring
our on the dazzle, vision
his element: acting a better
piece than he ever wrote. Found
tangled in eelgrass, days later,
less than his thumbed Keats or his last wife's ring.

IV. *Berlioz 1830*

You are Prince Hamlet, you are
a beetle coffined in black, one white
hand thrust in the stained waistcoat
to the heart. Ophelia
comes out, sees you, but does not
scream. . . . The applause rolls over
you, blood hollows in your ear;
your flight declines to a rout
into the wings, then the street's
ten degrees of frost, your skin
on fire with it: your skull
in your hands, and your hands freezing
sullenly. . . . Snow on your boots
crawls, the lamp's million worms of gold.

V. *For Osip Mandelstam*

He carries his head in a suitcase;
it is still smiling.

The prison guards bow,
they too smile;

they say, *Don't forget the gold teeth
are always gold.*

That's true, he admits, and empties them:
shells from a revolver.

Wait a minute, they call,
there's also your eyes.

I can see that, he shouts: *a pair of dice
to your luck, gentlemen!* and he flings them.

What a fine pair of ears, one murmurs,
and such clever nostrils. . . .

The ears are clipped, the nose slit:
it's a celebration.

And Osip, since you're leaving, they chuckle
remember—you aren't.

Can't hear you, gentlemen, the tongue taps in its skull;
can't hear you, now, at all.

The Source
(For Louis Coxe)

Your poems read me a man
who has been far, yet stayed alive at home
keeping things up: the wildflower meadows trimmed
decently each year, and all the goods of the house
uncluttered, easily found in place.

I dreamed we talked by your old carpenter's bench
freighted with tools: you held each slowly to the light
for a file and polish. Absorbed, but conversing well
"Now, some say the heart is in the wood"—your words
suddenly drifting like smoke on the air between us.

Since then, I have kept more watchful
even around the house; as you said
between words, a good piece of work is hard to find,
and with no telling beforehand what it will mean.

Union Cavalry on Leave
(Summer 1864)

Returning slowly up the long afternoons,
Eye and mouth gone slack as the hands on reins,
These horsemen drift in a haze of beginning summer;
Only some furious woodpecker for a drummer.

A door slams somewhere, behind a retreating back;
One trooper suddenly makes his roan's head jerk
And her feet boil sideways across the dust
That spreads beyond the road in a white rust.

There have gone so quietly now out of the War
So many this way, those waiting have slept past care
To arrive at a tight mouth and narrowed eye.
From behind windows, they watch each column die

Into the corners of dusk and the June heat,
Nor hear as louder than crickets the laconic feet
Passing forever, it seems, into the dark
While a mad bird perseveres at the stunned bark.

Weapons
(Three Family Portraits)

I. *Great-Great-Grandfather at Gettysburg*

Tongue-loll: the sweat
drains back to your canteen,
but the blood does not
find again its body. . . .

                    Michael Shea,
once a Grand Banks fisherman
and ne'er-do-well, somehow become
lance corporal of the First Maine
Volunteers:

            you unskewered
your man, maybe to ease him
"for the last minute
ever he was going to see
this earth" as you wrote
the homefolk. . . .

                Your bayonet
pegged on my wall, you're
eighty years dead
of TB and backcountry
winters, but the blade
keeps you alive:

                iron
at the core still, if a bit
rusty where you once tried
to clean with mud stains
the others, red.

II. *Meuse-Argonne Campaign, 1918*

"God, Great-uncle Frank's
gone and done it:
                    the fat-assed
drummer come home
from Frisco and run
right into the army, got
sent to France, was shot
in the pants, plugged
the leak with spare tobacco
and kept on chewing, saw
'a nice piece of cutlery'
was a ten-inch-blade
trench knife by a goner
Boche, and bit on it
clear to the dressing station.

Well, do you want to hear
he kicked off from absorbed
nicotine poisoning? Well,
he did."

        Frank, this thing
sure comes in handy, opening aerograms
from my girl in Heidelberg:

"the Raining her iss not so good
without You!"

III. *I. M. Lt. Neal Walker, USA, 1919-1944*

They don't send a battery of twin ack-acks
home with the mended laundry and the spare

boots, the commendation papers, medals,
and old camp dance programs you used

to clean your pipes with. They send home a portrait
photo, creased where the sniper's bullet went past

on its way in (they don't send home the shirt
half of which ended up in your lung).

                             Uncle Neal,
your old Springfield twenty-two shadows my wall

where you left it, cleaned and oiled, one spring day
of '44 after pinking at robber woodchucks

(we still have the buggers; they steal our corn
by night, and sometimes at noon; I have shot

at them, but lacking your good eye and quick finger
usually missed).
                I wonder if on Luzon,

taking it from all sides, your battery
wished to hell you hadn't got it—trying

to land the damn ack-acks through the surf
and slap of mortars, off-key whine of small arms

arching Hell over Leyte Gulf. "Oh God, that sure
sounds awful" some Tennessee corporal wails

just by your ear, and you tell him "Son, it sounds
almost like home" as the slug tears home and you

begin your thirty-year journey, hunched in time,
to end up this rifle sighting-in my life.

Fragment from a Last Letter Home
(Fall 1944)

Dear Cliff,

       is Father still living
in the breath of his apple trees,

in the bee's hum and blossom
rising at six

to cull the rottens, curb the scurrying worm?
How does Mother stand it—

does she hug the late moonlight to her
for a man?

       How long before

someone in that house cuts loose—the sickle
in the Old Man's groin, our corporate

bloody hand? . . .

Hunting Lessons

I. *A Memory of My Grandfather*
                (G. W. W., 1884-1964)

"For deer, you need somethin' heavy;
take this Winchester here:
thirty-eight caliber, fifty-five grain
soft nose—she'll spread
right through a doe 'n come out
the other side so big,
you can put your fist in 'er.
Boy, *you* try it."

                I was ten, my shoulder
half dropped off from the kick, and now
your season has closed.

II. *What My Ancestors Taught Me*

"Your first time, cleaning a buck, feels like
you've ripped the world apart: like
you could stick your hand out and search
right into its side. . . ."

Old Fathers who in my words
talk yourselves blue, forgive; tell me
once more what cold steel's for:

                        "Not
some easy story on a page, but the small lead ball
of truth under your tongue—

or an arm
leaning to scour the knifeblade off in sand."

My Grandfather's Wooden Planes

Block, boat, and edge; "sawhandle" and doubleblader,
their oak or maple, cherry or curling apple,
now fill my hands. I polish them with oil
and love, till my palms glisten with it— stained
forever. Till around me, the air
grows resinous with age (Old Man, you made things well
I don't want to do ill . . .).

                The glint of metal
watches, draws blood from the grain of my hand.

IV: *Fathering*

Herewith I solemnly renounce my hoard
of earthly goods, whatever counts as chattel.
The genius and guardian angel of this place
has changed to an old tree-stump in the water.

—Anna Akhmatova, "There Are Four of Us"
    (trans. Stanley Kunitz)

Final Postscript: For My Father

I used to create you intricate
like silver;
but the people we write that way
die on us
before we have lived them.

So I ask you back:
tarnish—do what you like
on my tumbledown shelf.

I am whispering this curse
for both of us.

Seasons of Passage

I. *Memory of My Ancestors in Midwinter*

After dark.... I walk out to the orchard:
black clouds hurl past, stripping the apple trees
to their gray bones.
                    Turning back to the house,
I steer by the window's orange beacon—faint
as old men burning against the night.

As I watch, the snow before me
thickens with their blood. And I remember
how my arms ached, wrestling those stones
they set, once, in my path.

II. *Vision in Early Summer*

I'm driving across the field
when suddenly a flaw troubles my sight:
not the sunset, and not even
lovely like blood.
                    I see the grass
caught up in the white fork of lightning,
cattle become charcoal and trees
strewing clinker like blossom.
                    I keep on
till I can't see to drive—then get out
stumbling: praying aloud I may reach
my unborn sons.

III.   *Fall Lines for My Wife, on My Thirtieth Birthday*

Cemetery hill.... I stand
Alone at dusk while a rising wind
Savages at the grass, pulls down
The sky's far corners....
                              Harvest once more
Is over: the fruitful season, ground
Again to ash and dust, may scour
These toppled stones clean past their prayers
And names, for my part.
                              Once I sang
Them upright, only to keep from falling
Myself; but that's how many years
And countries, Love, ago? ...
                              I swear
Wind and stone to silence now, and summon
More darkness than the dead could leave
To grow here—or more light. I move
Beside you, Love, and vow to carve
Our names with but half their dates: to dare
The future in lines lean as air.

In August

Harvests
have fallen inward: their blond dust
works under my thumbnail, under
the creases of my eyelids
become transparent.
A citron cloud
bruises the near hills.

We are two foxes, Love,
crying together—
shivering
in this heat where the last
wagon wheel, flung
a century back in the long grass,
is keeping dumb:

its wood spokes—
no longer
touching the hopes of the earth—
are powder;
its iron hub
a dark zero, burrowing
back to stone.

Three Dreams
(For M.)

I. *Mare Night*

Pacing my sleep, the horses
dance through your foreign shadow:

their sweat a sunfleck,
a flash of Caribbean coral,

and their eloquent breathing
a sunset of brown gauze—

our little horizon.

II. *Private Beach*

Afterbeat of hooves, leaving us
on our knees as though just born. An anger
of sand surrounds us, and coils; you strip off
the bikini, your shivering breasts are wrung
lillies on the wind—that fumbling, white hand
of vacancy, salt . . .
                    now your long hair
shaken out, soundlessly lashing the spray.

III. *The Guilt*

All night to reach the cloud-stalion,
the soot of his mane,

I had to grasp hand over hand
the pine boughs laddering my family hills.

I escaped
while they arrested you in my place.

Two Poems for an Anniversary

I. *Water: Des Images*

After years of rain, to fall
back to the child's dry well without a prayer
of climbing out alone . . .
                              then to feel
your tongue on my spine: small animal like water
splitting the rock.

II. *Stoic Epigram*

Ten years now, it's as though we've been two bowls
poured in and out of each other:
chipped, cracked; and accepting the hour
we sense waits in the wings, still whole,
to strike its verdict of beyond repair.

Three for a New Daughter

I. *A Prayer, A Welcome*

Little wrinkle
from my flesh, eyelid

curling down at my fool's
prattle; child

before whom I'm the more
child—your future

older than my past. . . .
Forgive the father

I'll be, become all
I can never know;

teach me to hold
you for a while, and then

to let go.

II. *The Beast of Burden*

My weight, suddenly increased
by your preposterous sixteen pounds,
starts to bow me down.

Your wise mother carried you
low; but I must bear you,
it seems, somehow firmly

on my shoulders (thus
the sins of the fathers
receive their lovely wages).

—And now you've clapped your hands
over my eyes, you're shouting
in my ears: enough to deafen

this already blind and dumb
staggerer who totes you, enfant
terrible beating time on my head,

into our separate futures.

III.   *The Naming*
                    (Emma Shea Jewett Walker)

Old names we dress you in, like
family heirlooms, celebrate
marriages that never were:

the Irish Sheas, once madcap
bogtrotters, domesticate
at last with the Jewetts'

lace indifference to the mob;
while the wool-raw Walkers, leaning
on pitchforks too clean for use,

look on wincing back their smiles. . . .
As for your daily self, worn
hand-me-down from certain novels'

heroines: may you be spared
their ball-dress-world dilemmas
if not your own.

         There now: starched,
ruffed, and pleated, and we hope
turned out in style—Pardon, dear,

our selfish taste that clothed you
against change. As we'll forgive the day
when, sure of your choice in names,

you leave us ours outgrown.

For Emma, at Sunrise

Foreign in sleep, your mother
turns from your cries that swallow
cold air for breath. Love is
how we hurt each other.

I sit in the dark, pretend
to comfort you—both of us
clinging to nothing, even
our heartbeats become stone.

Daughter, the world is now
and as it is. . . . We learn
together, watching the sun's
blind rise into silence.

Reflections on Proverbs
(Being Some Irreverent Future Advice for My Daughter)

Burning instead of beauty waits
The girl in time, the prophet found:
All whom their sin emancipates
Cleansed by the blueness of a wound. . . .

Outside the gate the prophet, howling,
Condemns the wine and spice within;
My daughter, take heed that your dwelling
Be soundproof, or you thick of skin.

Begin with pride: indifferent
To graybeards grumbling at short skirts,
And toward your spouse impenitent
For piles of still-unlaundered shirts.

Go hard of eye when shallow vision
Enlists the faith of every friend;
Though they decry cold indecision,
Gall shall breed honey in the end.

Love is a vineyard: if you browse there,
Study the vintage—lest you get
The lees too many who carouse there
Find wormwood in their glass. And yet,

Be married all your lifetime lightly;
Nor was that child of David young
Who sang of love feasts varied nightly—
Their Grace like manna, tongue to tongue.

For My Daughter before Dawn

Her only weight herself, she sleeps
Dreamless who'll wake to cry for food....
I hear the dogs cry: something leaps
In the night that is not up to good.

Even awake, I dream of deer
Stunned in the thicket of their need:
Of the torn sinew, the mangled ear
Softer than moss; of the wasted seed....

I dream the hounds that, waking, plunge
Across the dark by an inner light;
By day, this hand could make them cringe
For a bone tossed careless from my plate....

My daughter stirs, hearing my hand
Approach: a gesture, like the sun,
From the white, enormous owner trained
To feed her till her time to run.

About the Series

Moving Out is the first collection in a series established by Virginia Commonwealth University and sponsored jointly by VCU, the Associated Writing Programs, and the University Press of Virginia. *Moving Out* was selected from more than a thousand collections solicited nationally by the editorial board of the Associated Writing Programs, and read by twenty-three poets and critics from throughout the country. The preliminary readers were Harry Antrim, John Ashbery, Kay Cassill, Bruce Cutler, Robert Day, R. H. W. Dillard, George Garrett, James B. Hall, William Hathaway, Edward Lueders, James McAuley, Howard McCord, William Peden, Roger Rath, Richard Shelton, John C. Stewart, George Starbuck, William Tremblay, Ray B. West, James P. White, John Williams, Miller Williams, and R. V. Williams. A smaller group of poets, comprised of R. H. W. Dillard, George Garrett, James B. Hall, William Peden, James Whitehead, and Miller Williams screened the 126 manuscripts judged by the readers to be of excellent quality, and recommended fourteen to Richard Eberhart as finalists. Mr. Eberhart selected *Moving Out* to receive the VCU Series award, and cited four other collections by Robert Huff, Richard Moore, David Posner, and Leon Stokesbury as superior books. *Moving Out* was edited by Walton Beacham in conjunction with the author. At least one volume of poems is published annually; manuscripts are invited in the fall of each year.

About the Author

David Walker was born in Maine in 1942. He is a graduate of Bowdoin College and of Oxford University, where he was a Fulbright Scholar at New College. He has taught at several universities and has traveled extensively in Europe and the Pacific (including three years spent in New Zealand).

His poems have been published in such magazines as *Poetry*, the *New Yorker*, the *Antioch Review, Transatlantic Review,* the *Poetry Review* (London), and *Landfall* (New Zealand).

At present he lives with his wife and small daughter on a farm in Alna, Maine, which has belonged to his family since 1780. He is working on a new collection of poems and some fiction.